This book belongs to:

_____

In Loving Memory of My Mum

This story is written with love and deep gratitude in memory of my mum, who was my guiding light, my comfort, and my inspiration. Just like Nanny Tina, she filled my life with joy, warmth, and magical moments that I will cherish forever. Though she may no longer be by my side, I feel her presence in every twinkling star, gentle breeze, and colorful rainbow.

Mum, your love continues to wrap around me like a cozy blanket, giving me the strength to explore the world with courage and a smile. I know you are watching over me from your fluffy cloud, cheering me on with pride. This story is a reflection of the beautiful and everlasting love you gave me, a love that, like a boomerang, always comes back.

Thank you for being my guardian angel, now and forever.

Lenny's Sparkly Guardian Angel

By Charlene Marvell

Chapter 1: The Super-Fun Nanny

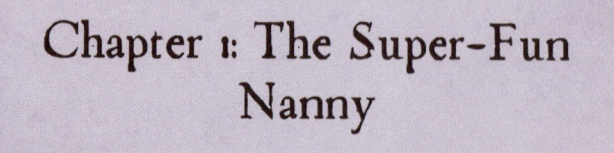

Lenny had the coolest nanny ever! Her name was Tina, and she was like a magical fairy godmother. Nanny Tina read the most exciting bedtime stories, played silly games, and took Lenny on super-duper adventures. When Nanny Tina was around, Lenny felt as happy as a kid in a candy store!

Chapter 2: The Big Uh-Oh

One day, Nanny Tina got really sick and couldn't come play anymore. Lenny felt super sad, like his favorite toy was lost forever. But then, Lenny's family told him something amazing - Nanny Tina had become a sparkly guardian angel to watch over him from the fluffy clouds above!

Chapter 3: The Twinkle-Twinkle Star

One night, Lenny saw the brightest, sparkliest star ever in the sky. It winked at him like it was playing peekaboo! Lenny remembered how Nanny Tina loved stargazing, and it made him feel all warm and fuzzy inside.

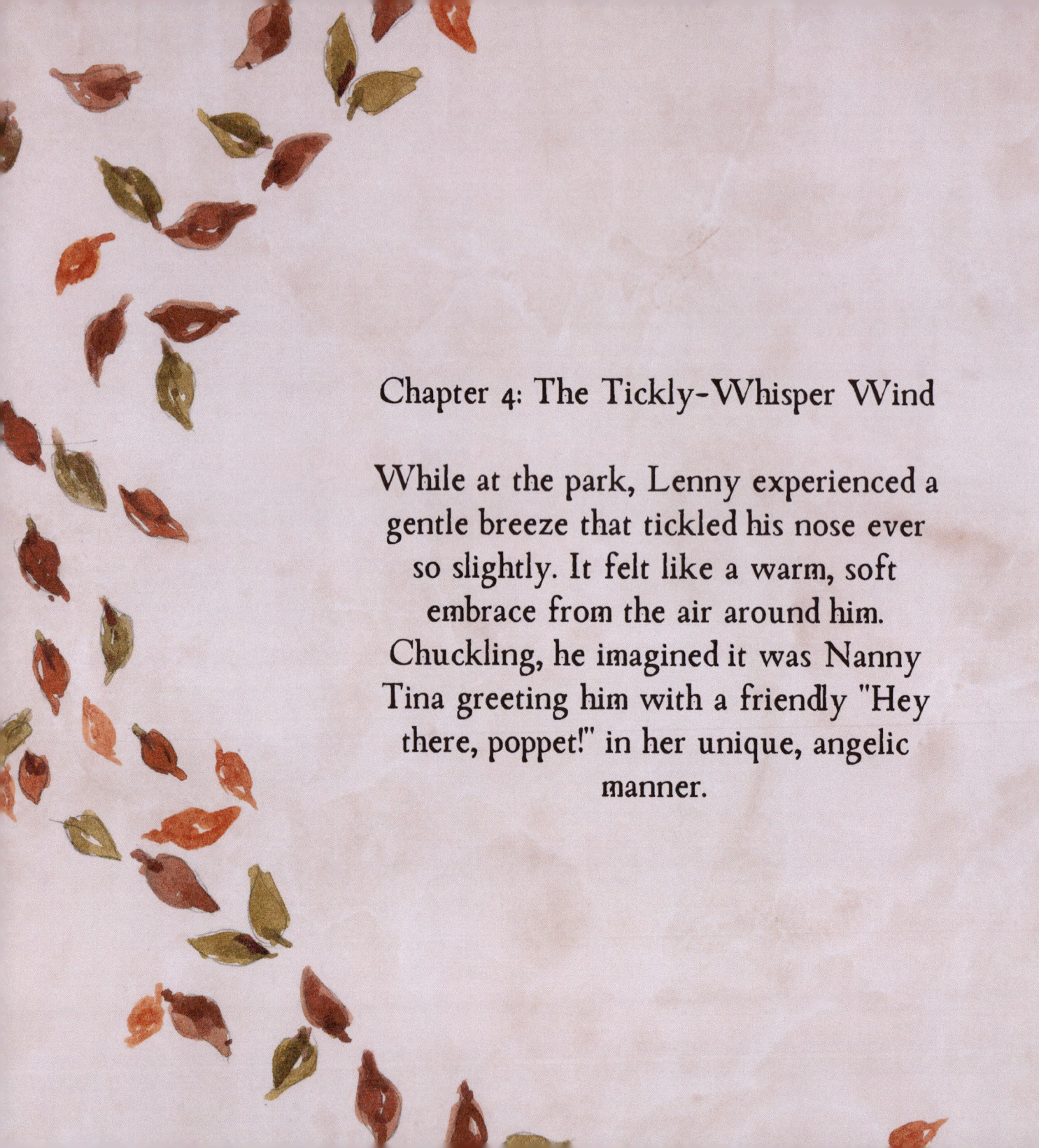

Chapter 4: The Tickly-Whisper Wind

While at the park, Lenny experienced a gentle breeze that tickled his nose ever so slightly. It felt like a warm, soft embrace from the air around him. Chuckling, he imagined it was Nanny Tina greeting him with a friendly "Hey there, poppet!" in her unique, angelic manner.

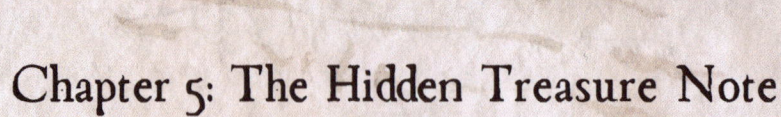

Chapter 5: The Hidden Treasure Note

Lenny found a secret note in his favorite storybook. It said, "Whenever you need a hug, just look around - I'm right here, giving you an invisible squeeze!" Lenny smiled so big, his cheeks hurt!

Chapter 6: The Super-Duper Rainbow

After a rainy day, Lenny saw the most colorful rainbow ever - it looked like a giant candy necklace in the sky! He remembered Nanny Tina saying rainbows were magic messages of love, and he felt like she sent this one just for him.

Chapter 7: The Snuggly Angel Blanket

Lenny's Mum gave him a special blanket covered in pictures of Nanny Tina. It was so soft and cozy, like being wrapped in a cloud! Lenny cuddled with it every day, feeling like Nanny Tina was giving him a big bear hug.

Chapter 8: The Brave Little Explorer

Whenever Lenny felt scared or sad, he'd look for signs from Nanny Tina - twinkling stars, tickly breezes, or pretty rainbows.

Knowing his guardian angel was watching made him feel brave enough to try new things and have lots of fun!

Chapter 9: Sharing the Angel Secret

Lenny was so excited about his guardian angel that he told all his friends at school. During playtime, he gathered them around and shared how Nanny Tina watched over him from the clouds, sending twinkling stars, tickly breezes, and magical rainbows as signs of her love. His friends listened in awe, amazed by Lenny's special connection with his angel. Lenny felt proud and happy to share Nanny Tina's love with them.

Chapter 10: Forever and Ever

As Lenny grew bigger and taller, he always remembered Nanny Tina's love.

He knew she was cheering him on from her fluffy cloud, proud of every new thing he learned.

The End (But Not Really!)

Lenny's story shows us that love is like a boomerang - it always comes back to us! Even when we can't see someone we love, their love is still all around us, giving us invisible hugs and making us smile.

Dear Awesome Reader,

Wow! You just finished Lenny's magical story! Wasn't that super cool?

Remember, even if you can't see someone you love, their love is still all around you - just like Nanny Tina's was for Lenny. It's like having your very own invisible superhero!

Next time you see a twinkly star, feel a tickly breeze, or spot a colourful rainbow, maybe it's your own guardian angel saying "Hi there!" They might even be doing a silly dance right now, just to make you giggle!

You're super special and always loved. Your guardian angel is probably giving you a big, squishy hug right this second! Can you feel it?

Keep being amazing, and don't forget to look for the magic all around you!

Big smiles and angel high-fives,
Your friend, Charlene

Fun Activities:

Draw a Picture of Your Own Guardian Angel: Using the opposite page.

Make a List of 5 Things That Make You Feel Happy and Safe: Just like Lenny's angel signs.

Create a Special "Angel Box": To keep treasures that remind you of someone you love.

Go on a Rainbow Scavenger Hunt: Find something red, orange, yellow, green, blue, and purple!

Have a Stargazing Picnic: With your family, and make up funny names for the constellations.

Guess what? You've got a super-special guardian angel, just like Lenny! They're always watching over you with a big smile. Right now, your angel might be sprinkling sparkly star dust or painting invisible rainbows just for you. Remember, you're wrapped in cozy angel hugs all day long!

Fun Questions to Ponder:

If you had a guardian angel like Nanny Tina, what fun game would you want to play with them?

If your guardian angel could give you a magical power for one day, what power would you choose?

If you could design a special blanket like Lenny's, what pictures or patterns would you put on it?

What's your favourite way to remember someone special who isn't around anymore?

If you saw a star winking at you like it did for Lenny, what would you wish for?

What's the silliest thing you think guardian angels do when no one is looking?

If your guardian angel could turn into any animal to play with you, what animal would you pick?

Remember, there are no right or wrong answers! Let your imagination soar like a guardian angel and have fun thinking about these magical ideas!

Printed in Great Britain
by Amazon